Normee Ekoomiak

ARCTIC MEMORIES

Henry Holt and Company • New York

Thanks to Lillian Robinson, Dr. Brian Dobbs, Bela Kalinovits, Phil Surguy, Leo Flaherty, Rolf Roemer, Katolic Utatnaq, the Baffin Divisional Board of Education, the Ontario Arts Council, the Canada Council, and the Multiculturalism Sector of the Department of the Secretary of State of Canada, without whose help this book would never have been published.

Library of Congress Cataloging-in-Publication Data
Ekoomiak, Normee. Arctic memories / Normee Ekoomiak. English and Eskimo.
Summary: Text in both Inuktitut and English describes a now vanished way of life for the Inuit.
ISBN 0-8050-1254-0 1. Eskimos—Juvenile literature. 2. Eskimo language—Texts—Juvenile literature.
[1. Eskimos. 2. Eskimo language materials—Bilingual.] I. Title.
E99.E7E38 1990 998'.004971—dc20   89-39194

Henry Holt books are available at special discounts for bulk purchases for sales promotions, premiums, fund-raising, or educational use. Special editions or book excerpts can also be created to specification.

For details contact:

Special Sales Director
Henry Holt and Company, Inc.
115 West 18th Street
New York, New York 10011

ARCTIC MEMORIES

NORMEE EKOOMIAK.

ᐃᒡᓗ ᐃᓗᐊᓂ

ᓄᑕᖄᐅᔪᕐᔪᐊᕐᔪᖕ ᐃᒡᓗᒥᓯᒪᔪᕐᓚᐅᕐᔪᖕ ᐅᑭᐅᖅᑎᓪᓗᒍ ᐊᒻᒪᓗ ᐅᑭᐅᖅᑐᖅᓕᕆᖅᓯᒃ ᑐᐱᕐᒥᒡᓕᕐᔪᓇᑦ. ᐃᒡᓚᓄᐅᑦᑕᑉᑐᑦ ᐃᖅᑐᐊᖅᑐᑐᐅᑦᓯᖕᒃ ᐊᐳᕐᑦᓘ. ᐅᑭᐅᖅᑕᒥᓂᒥ ᓯᓇᔪᖇᖅᑑᖕ ᐅᑭᐅᖕᑯᑦᖄ. ᐃᒃᑳᓇᕐᓯᓄ ᐊᒻᒪᓗ ᑖᖅᓗᓄᓯ. ᓯᖅᓯᓂᖕ ᑕᐊᖅᖃᕐᑕᖅᑦ ᑭᕐᐊᓯᓂᖕ ᐅᐱᖅᓴᒃᔪᖅᖅᐊᕐᕐᒃ, ᖅᑐᐅᑐᔦᐊᕐᓯᓄᕃᖕ ᐅᓂᕐᑦᔭᓕᓄᓱᖅᔅ ᐅᑭᐅᖅᑐᔅᖅᖅᖕ ᐊᓯᓐᕐᖄᐅᑎᔪᕃᖕ ᑭᕆᐊᓯᓄ ᐱᓕᓂᕐᑦᔪᑎ ᖅᑎᓄᕐᔪᓄᓗ ᐃᒡᓗ ᐃᒡᔪᐊᓂ. ᐅᕈᕐ ᐊᑕᐊ ᓴᓇᖅᔪᐊᕐᑑᖕ ᐅᖅᓯᕈ ᓴᓇᖅᔪᐊᔅᖄᒥ ᓄᐅᐱᖅᑕᑐᕐᐊᕐᓯᓱᕐᖕ. ᐅᕈᕐ ᐊᔦᓂ ᒣᖅᔪᖅᑐᖕ ᓇᔪᕇᐅᑦ ᐊᒻᕐᓯᓄᐅᑉ ᑐᐊᑎᑐᑉᕆᓯᓄᒥ. ᐅᖅᖅᐅᕐᖄᓂᓯ ᑕᐊᕐᑦᕐᖄᖕ ᑕᐊᕐ ᑐᐃᕐᖕ. ᐃᒡᓗ ᐃᒡᔪᐊᓂ ᖅᑐᕐᖕ ᓄᐅᖅᖅᖅᔅ ᐱᓂᕈᖅᓄᕐᖕ. ᑕᐊᕐᓄ ᑕᐊᕐᑦᕐᖄᖅᑦ ᖅᑐᕐᖕ ᐊᒻᒪᓗ ᐅᖅᓯᖅᑮᕐᖄᕐᔅᓄ ᓇᕐᕐᒃᕐᓯᕐᑦ. ᓯᓄᖅᑲᓐᓇᐊᑦ ᖅᑐᕐᖕ ᖅᕃᑦᑐᕐᖅᖄᕐᓯᓄ ᐃᒡᓗ ᐅᖅᑐᐊᕐᐊᑦᓄᕐᑦᖄᕐᖕ. ᖅᐱᓯᖅᑮᖅᖄᓄᑦ ᔪᑦᔅ ᐊᕈᖅᓇᓄᕐᑦ ᑖᒃᐊ ᐅᖅᖅᔪᐊᑦ ᓄᑕᖅᕐ ᐅᖅᖄᓄᓯᓄᕐᒤᕐᑦ ᐃᓇᖅᓇᔪᑦ ᓯᕐᕐᑕᐋᒻ ᐊᕐᐅᕐᓯᕐᖄᕐᓇᕐᑦ ᐊᑦᐊᓇᕐᓯᕐᕐᓯᒍᐊᓗᓯᒍᓚᑦ.

In the Iglu

"Iglu" means house. When I was small, we used to live in a snow house in the winter and in a tent the rest of the year. During the long winter up North, there is little sun and it is always dark. We stay inside and do our work and play. Here the father is carving a soapstone sculpture for sale at the co-op. The mother is sewing together seal skins to cover a tent. When it starts to get warm, the snow house will melt. We will build a tent to live in, and we will move with it from place to place when we hunt for food. Inside the iglu there is an oil lamp on three legs. It is for light and for heat. But when we go to sleep, we put out the lamp, and then it gets cold, so we must all sleep together to keep warm. The kids sleep in the middle, between their parents.

ᐅᑭᐅᖅᑕᖅᑐᒥ ᐅᐱᓐᖓᒥ

ᑐᕝᕕᓕᕋᖓᑦ ᐊᒻᒪᓗ ᑎᒃᑕᐅᔾᔭᐅᓗᓂ ᓯᕿᓂᕐᒧᑦ. ᑎᕝᒥᐊᑦ ᑎᑭᐸᓪᓕᐊᓗᑎᒃ ᐅᑭᐅᖅᑕᖅᑐᒧᑦ ᐃᕿᕿᓕᐅᓇᐊᑐᕐᓗᑎᒃ. ᑎᕝᒥᐊᑦ ᐅᑭᐅᖅᑕᖅᑐᒥᐅᑕᑎᑐᑦ ᓂᕿᓴᕝᕕᑦ ᐊᒻᒪᓗ ᐃᕿᕿᓕᐊᓗᑎᒃ ᐱᐊᓛᒥᕐᓂᒃᓗ ᐱᕈᖅᓴᔾᔪᐃᑦ. ᓂᓚᕿᒃᑐᑦ ᑕᓯᕐᕋᒥᑦ ᐊᒻᒪᓗ ᐃᒋᐱᒃᓴᒐᕐᓂᑦ ᓄᓇᒥ.

ᓇᓄᖅ ᑳᒃᑐᖅ ᓂᕿᒥᑦ ᕿᓂᖅᑐᖅ. ᐊᓇᓇᖓ ᓇᑦᓯᖅ ᐅᖃᐅᑎᓪᓗᓂᐅᒃ ᓇᑦᓯᐊᖓ ᓇᓗᖁᓪᓗᓂᐅᒃ ᐅᐃᒪᐃᔭᑦᓯᐊᓗᓂ. ᓇᓄᖅ ᓂᕆᔪᒪᑐᐃᓐᓇᖅᑐᖅ ᓇᑦᓯᕐᒥᑦ ᑭᓯᐊᓂ ᓂᕆᔪᓐᓇᕐᑕᐃ ᐃᖃᓗᐃᑦ ᐊᓯᕝᕕᓂᒃᓗ ᐃᒪᕐᒥᐅᑕᓂᑦ ᐆᒪᔪᓂᑦ.

Arctic Spring

The ice is breaking up, getting ready to float across James Bay. It will soon be summer, and the Canada geese are flying north to lay eggs to make more Canada geese. If they are born in the South, they are not as healthy. There is too much pollution, and they do not have the right food. They like the North because it's natural for them.

Nanook, the polar bear, is hungry and is looking for food. The mother seal calls the baby seal, and they swim away and are safe. Now the bear has to eat fish. He would like to eat seal, but if he eats too much of it, he will get wild. It is better for bears to eat fish most of the time. Then they can be our friends.

NORMEE EKOOMIAK

ᕿᑎᒃᑐᑦ ᐊᒋᐅᑉᐱᓐᓂᕐᒥ

ᕿᑎᒍᒪᑦᑕᖅᑐᒍᑦ ᓯᓚᒥ. ᑕᑉᕙ ᐊᑕᑕᖓ ᕿᑎᖅᑲᑕᐅᔪᖅ ᐸᓂᖕᒥᓂᒃ ᐊᒻᒪᓗ ᐱᖓᓱᑦ ᐃᕐᓂᖏᑦ ᐊᒋᐊᑉᐱᓐᓂᕐᒥ. ᓯᓚᒥ ᕿᑎᒃᐸᒃᑯᕕᑦ ᑎᒦᑦ ᖃᓄᖅ ᐃᖏᓂᖅᑲᑦᓯᐊᕋᔭᖅᓂᖓᓄᑦ ᐊᒻᒪᓗ ᓱᖏᑦᓯᐊᓗᓂ.

ᐃᒡᓗᖅᑲᖅᑐᓂ ᐊᐳᒻᒥᑦ ᐅᖁᑦᑎᐊᖅᑐᖅ ᐃᓗᐊᓂ. ᐱᖅᓯᐊᓂᒃᑳᖓᑦ ᐊᐳᑕᐃᔭᖅᓗᒍ ᐹᖓ ᑭᓯᐊᓂ ᐊᓂᓇᖅᑐᖅ.

Playing on a Snowbank

We love to go outside and play. Here three boys and a girl are playing with their father on a snowbank. They all slide down, and then race to get back to the top and do it all over again.

Inside an iglu there is not very much space. You cannot stay inside for a long time, not even during a snowstorm. But if you go outside to play, then your body will always be healthy and normal.

Also, someone has to go outside the iglu after a snowstorm to dig the people out.

NORMEE EKOOMIAK.

ᓯᑯᒥ ᐃᖃᓗᑦᑕᐊᕐᓂᖅ

ᐃᓚᓄᖅᑯᑦ ᐱᖅᐸᓂᖅᐳᖅᓇᖕ ᐅᑕᕐᖕᑦ ᑕᑯᑕ ᑐᒃᑐᐃᑦ, ᓇᐲᖕ ᐊᕐᓗ ᐊᐃᐱᑦ ᓇᓇᖕᓂᖅ ᐊᕐᔭᓇᖏᑐᐃᑦ. ᓂᖅᐱᑦᖃᖃᑎᒍ ᑭᕐᐊᓂ ᐱᑕᖃᖕᓯᓇᖅᓇᖕᑦ ᐃᖃᓗᖕᐸᑎᐳᖅᖃᑐᒍᑦ. ᐊᖃᓗᐊᑎᐅᖅᖃᑕᑐᐸᖕᑦ ᐃᖃᓗᖕᓗᕐᖃᖃᓯᑎᖕᑦ ᐃᖃᓗᖕᐱᖕᓂᖅ.

ᐊᕐᓇᓯᖃᖕ ᑕᖃᓇᓇᖕ ᐃᒪᖃᓇᖕ ᑲᐳᕐᓗ ᐃᖃᓗᖕᖅᐲᖅᓯᖅᐊᖅᐊᖅᖃᓇᖕᑦ. ᑭᕐᐊᓂ ᐃᓚᓄᖅᑯᑦ ᐃᖃᓗᖕᖅᐱᖕᓇᖕᑐᖅ.

ᐅᑕᕐᖃᑲᓴᓄᖃᖕ ᓂᖅᐱᓯᖕᑎᓂᖕᓂ ᓄᒥ ᑐᐱᖃᐱᖃᖃᑎ ᐊᕐᐸᖅᐸᓯᕐᖅᖃᑐᐃᑦ. ᐊᕐᒍᓇᔪᖃᑦ ᓯᔪᓇᖕᑐᖕᑦ ᖃᑐᐱᒪᖃᖅᑐᐃᑦ ᓇᓇᓗᖃᖃᑦ ᐅᑕᕐᐊᑦ.

Ice Fishing

After a snowstorm it is hard to find caribou and seal and walrus. All of the birds and animals are gone. Sometimes months go by before they come back. So the whole family has to go out fishing, to catch the arctic char, through holes in the ice. Sedna is good, and she makes sure there are plenty of fish. But sometimes it is hard to catch any fish, and the birds and animals stay away for a long time. Then the people must move to a new camp if they are strong enough. Or else they will starve.

ᐅᑲᐱᒃ - ᐱᒃᑐᕐᐱ

ᐅᑲᐱᒃ ᐅᖅᑲᖅᑕᐅᔨᖅ ᐃᓄᒃᑐᑦ. ᑕᒐ ᐃᓚᕆᔭᕐᒃ ᐃᑲᔪᖅᑕᖅᓱᓂ ᒥᐊᓂᖅᑐᒃᐹ ᐅᕝᕙᓕᓂᖅ ᐅᐱᐅᖅᑕᒍᖅᒥ. ᐅᕐᓂ ᑕᑯᖕᑎᑦ ᐅᑲᐱᒃ ᐃᑲᔪᖅᑎᖃ ᓯᖅᖑᓐᓱ, ᑕᖅᓱ ᐊᒻᓗ ᐅᑦᓯᓯᐊᑦ. ᐊᐅᔭᖅᑐᖅᓱᑎᐅᒃ ᐊᑦᑎᖅᕐᓯᐅᕐᒃ ᐊᖑᒪᐊᕐᓂᓂᑎᓐᓱ ᖃᐅᕐᓯ ᐊᖕᕐᓱᓂ ᐊᒻᓗ ᖃᕈᒻᒥᓂᖅ . ᐊᓂᐱᕐᐅᖅᑦ ᐊᐅᔭᖅᑐᐃᖁᐅᖅᑕᐅᖅᑕᒃᔪᖅ ᓄᑕᓕᑕᒍᒃ ᐊᒻᖃᒻᒥᓐᓂᑦ ᐅᑲᐱᒃ ᒥᐊᓂᖅᔭᖅ ᐊᓂᖕ ᐊᒻᓗ ᑎᖕᕐᐊᒥᖅ. ᐅᕝᕙᓕᓂᖅ ᐃᑲᔪᖅᑎᑦ ᐃᑲᔪᖅᑎᖅᑐᐊᑦ ᐊᐅᔭᖅᑐᖅᓱᓐᓱ ᐅᐲᐅᖅᑐᔪᖅᑦ. ᖃᐱᐊᔪᖅᑎᕐᐊᖅᖅ⁶ᕐᔪᑦ ᐊᒻᓗ ᑐᖅᕐᑦᖅᓱᑦ ᓂᖅᑎᖕᑦᐊᕐᑦᐅᖅᓂᑦ ᑕᒐ ᐃᑲᔪᖅᑎᖅᕐᔪᑦ ᓂᖅᓂᖅ
ᓇᓂᔭᒐᖅᑕᐃᓪᓱᒍᐊᖁᓐᒍᑦ.

Okpik—The Lucky Charm

"Okpik" means "snowy owl." He is our friend, and his spirit protects all of nature in the North. Here you see the owl spirit, with the sun and the moon and the stars. He is watching over a father who is going hunting with his dog and spear, and he is watching over a mother with a baby in the hood of her *amautiq*. Okpik also is the guardian of the polar bear and of the geese. All of the nature spirits work together and watch over the North. We must keep them happy and only kill the right animals or else the spirits will not let us find food.

ᓂᒪ ⊲ᐅᶜᒥᑕ⊲ᖅᐸᖯ⊃ᖅ

ᐃᒪᑉᑭᒧ ᐱᐱᐅᖔᔨᕐᖅ. ᐅᒡᒻᖃ⊂ᐅᖯᕆᒧᖅ ᓂᖅᕆᑐᖯᐱᖅᓄᖓ ᒍᐱᓕᑌᔨᕗᓇᖓ. ᒪᒪᶜᒪ
ᓄᕆ⊲ᖯᒪᐅᔅᐅᒍ ᓄᒍᒻ ᒍᐱᓴᖯᕐᒪ ᖁᖅᖃᔨ⊲ᔪᖯ ⊲ᐸ⊲ᓄᶜ, ᒪᐃᒌᕖᶜ ᐅᖯᖮᖯᖯ⊃ᒍᶜ. ᓇᖯ⊲ᓄᐃᶜ
ᐃᓄᐃᶜ ᐃᓕᐅᖯᕐᒪᖯᒍᓐᖯ ᒪᒪ̇ᓂ ᓄᓇ ᖃᓄᒻ⊃ᓄᖯ ᐃᓄᖯᐱᕆ⊂ᐅᖯᕐᓄᶜ. ᓇᖯ⊲ᐃᶜ ᐃᒪᖯᓇᶜ ᐅᖯ᷒ᓄᖯ
ᓂᒪᖯᖯᓇᖮᖯᖅ ⊲ᐅᶜᒥᑕ⊲ᖯᒪᶜ ⊲ᒪᕐᓄᖯᓄᖯᶜ ᐅ̇ᒪᕖᶜᖮᒧ.

ᐃᒪᑉᑭᒧ ᐅᖮᐅᓄᶜ ⊲ᐱᖮᒍᕐᒪᒪᖯᖯᓄᒪᐅᖯᒪᶜ: ᖃᓇᒪᖯᖮᖯᔪᓇ, ᒲᖯᖯᖯᖮᖯᔪᓇ ⊲ᒪᔪ
ᓄᓇᕐ⊲ᖯᖮᖯᔪᓇ. ᐃᓄᐃᶜ ᐊᕐᒪᖯᕐᒪᐅᖯᖮᶜ ⊲ᐅᶜᒥᑕ⊲ᖯᖯᖅ ᓇᔪᒍᐃᓇᖅ. ᒪᐃᒪ̇ᒐᶜ ᐃᓄᐃᶜ
ᕐᒪᖯᕐ⊲ᖮ ᖃᖯᖱᒪ̇ᓄᖮᒍᶜ ᐅᖯᐅᕐᖮ᷒ᓄᶜ ᒍᖯᕐᒍᖯᐅᶜᒍᶜ.

The Body Needs to Travel

This happened a long time ago. There was no food near the village. The people had to travel to a new place, miles and miles across the ice of Hudson Bay. Half of the people did not want to go. They wanted to stay where they were born and grew up. But the other people said the body needs to travel. They had to find the right spot for themselves, where there would be more animals and birds and fish.

This took place thousands of years ago. There was no Canada and no Arctic Quebec and no Northwest Territories. This was how the Inuit went from one place to all of the other places. This is why all of the people who live around the North Pole can understand each other and why they speak languages that are almost the same.

Artist by Norman Ekoomiak.

ᐱᕐᓯᓕᐊᑦ

ᐅᐃᓐᖕᒐᒃᑯᑦ ᐊᒻᒪᓗ ᐊᐅᔭᒥᑦ ᐃᓄᐃᑦ ᐃᕐᑲᓗᒃᐸᒃᑐᑦ, ᐱᕐᓯᓕᐊᕆᔭᐅᓪᓗᑎᒃ ᓂᕿᖕᒐᑕᐅᕐᑲᑦᑕᖅᑐᑦ. ᐅᑭᐅᒃᑯᑦ ᕐᑯᐊᕆᔭᐅᓪᓗᑎᒃ ᑐᕐᑯᖅᓯᒪᑦᑎᐊᕐᓗᒋᑦ ᐱᔭᐅᑦᑕᐃᓚᒐᐅᒐᔭᕐᓂᖕᒐᓄᑦ ᓇᓄᕐᓄᑦ, ᐊᒪᕈᓄᑦ ᐊᒻᒪᓗ ᑎᕆᒐᓂᐊᕐᓄᑦ.

ᒥᐊᓂᕐᓯᔾ ᐅᒃᐱᒃ ᑕᑯᕗᖅ ᓇᓄᕐᒥᑦ ᕐᑲᐃᔪᒥᒃ ᐃᓂᖅᑎᓇᔭᖅᑐᕐᑐᖅ ᐃᓄᖕᓄᑦ. ᐃᕐᑲᓗᐃᑦ ᐃᑎᖅᓯᔭᕐᑐᕐᓗᑎᒃ ᐃᒡᓗᒧᑦ ᓇᓄᖅ ᑭᓯᐊᓂ ᓱᑕᐃᕐᐸᑦ.

Hanging Fish

After the fish have been caught, the people have to hang them up to dry and to freeze. They cannot leave the fish under the snow, or the polar bear or wolf or fox could find the fish and eat it.

Here the snowy owl sees the polar bear coming and warns the people. They take the fish with them inside the iglus and wait for the bear to go away. Then they will hang the fish up again.

Okpik watches over his people and makes sure that their food is safe.

NORMEE EKOOMIAK

ᐅᖅᑯᐊᖅ

ᐊᓄᕆᕐᓇᖦᐅᑕ ᓂᕐᔪᑎᑦ ᓂᕿᑐᒃᑭᑎᖕᓂ ᐊᖁᒐᕐᖐᐊᕐᔪᑦ
ᖁᓂᕐᑳᑑᑕᑦ ᐊᖁᒐᕐᖐᐊᕐᐅᕐᒐᕐᑐᓂ.
ᑕᖦᑐᐃᐊᖄᓐᕐᐊᕐᖕᒥᖅ ᐃᑦᓗᓀᐅᕐᑳᑐᑦ
ᓕᑦᖐᑦᐅᐸᖕᒐᖐᐊᕐᖕᒥᖄᕐ ᐃᑦᓗᓀᐅᕐᑳᑐᑦ, ᖃᕐᐊᓂ
ᓕᑦᐅᖕᖅᐅᕐᓂᖄᕐ ᐅᖅᕐᐊᒐᐅᐱᐊᓀᖕᓄᖅ ᖃᐊᕐᑳᑐᑦ
ᐊᑑᕐᓀᑦ.

ᐊᓄᕐᖕᓵᕐᖕᒥᕐᖦ ᑐᖐᖐᖕᖅᕐᖐᐊᕐᖦ ᐅᑎᓐᖐᖕᖅ ᐃᑕᒥᐅᖅ
ᐅᖅᖑᕐᐊᑐᕐᖅᑳᑐᖅ ᒪᕐᑐᖅ ᐊᖕᐅᑦ ᑕᒪᓇᖐᖦ ᐃᓄᐃᑦ
ᑐᖐᖃᑎᐱᐦᖕᖅ.

The Shelter

When it is hard to find animals and fish for
food, then the two best hunters in the village
go out to look for a better place. At the end
of the day, they build a shelter for the night.
If the weather is bad, they build a whole
iglu. But when the weather is not bad, all
they need is a windbreak made of two layers
of snow blocks. At the end of the next day
they build another shelter. This goes on
every day until the hunters find a good spot
for a new village. Then they go back home,
and soon the other Inuit, ten or twenty people, will move to a new place.

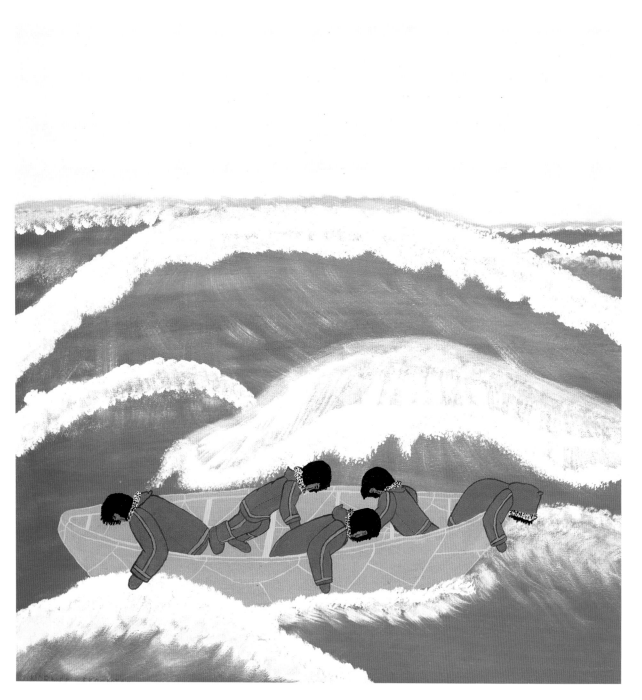

ᐱᕐᓗᒃᑕᐅᕐᒪᕐᕿᐊᑦ

ᑕᐃᕝᓗᓂᐅᖅ ᑕᐃᒃᑯᐊ ᐃᓅᖕᑑᑦ ᖄᐅᔭᖅᐅᒥᕋ
ᐱᖕᓄᐊᖃᓚᐅᐅᖕᒥᕐᓂᑦ. ᐃᓕᖅᐊᓕᖅᕆᒃ ᐱᕐᓗᒃᑕᐅᕐᐱᓚᓯᕐᑦ.
ᑕᒃᑯᐊ ᐃᓅᖕᑑᑦ ᐃᑭᓂᖕᑯᖕ ᐅᒥᐊᕐᒃ ᐊᒻᓗ
ᐅᕝᓚᕐᒃᑑᑦ ᐃᐱᓐᕐᑎᖕᑑᖕ ᑫᖃᑦᕐᒥᑎᐅᑎᑦ. ᓄᐊ
ᑕᑦᔮᐊᐃᖅᑐᒍ ᑭᔾᐊᓂ ᐊᑕᓂᔾᑐᐊᐊᓂᑦ
ᑕᑐᑕᑑᐊᓂᖕᑑᖕ. ᑕᒃᑯᐊ ᐃᕐᓂᓂᑑᖕ ᐸᑐᖕᐱᑦ, ᓂᖅᖕᐱᑦ
ᐊᒻᓗ ᐊᕐᖕᑕᓕ ᐱᕐᑎᖕᑎᑦ ᐃᓕᕐᑑᑦ. ᓇᓂᖅᐅᖕᓂᖕ
ᐱᖕᓗᓯᑦ ᐱᓇᕐᐊᑉᑉᑦ ᖃᖕᓕᕐᑦ, ᑐᔾᑕᖕᓗᖕᖃᓯᖕᓂᖕ
ᖃᖕᓂᑐᒐᑦᕐ.

The Curse

This is a true story. When an evil person learns your name, he can use your name when he does bad things. This is a terrible curse.

Once, some teenage boys went to school in the South. A bad man discovered their names, and then he committed crimes. The police came to arrest the boys and did not believe they were not guilty. So the boys went to jail for something they had not done. When they got out, they were sent back home. They told their parents what had happened. They had been beaten up and sent to jail. This was a terrible scandal and a shame and a curse.

So the boys had to die. They got into an *umiak* and went out into James Bay so far that they could no longer see the land but only the waves. Then they threw their paddles and their food and oil and their warm clothing over the side of the boat. They were found three weeks later. They had all starved to death.

NORMEE EKOOMIAK

ᖁᑭᖅᖁᓄ ᐊᖅᐸᕆᐊᖅᑕᖅᓂᖅ

ᐃᓄᐃᑦ ᖁᑎᒍᕆᓂᖅ ᐊᖅᕆᐊᖃᖅᒍᔭ ᓂᑕᖃᖅᐸᕿᐊᕿᖥ
ᐊᒻᓗ ᐱᓐᓇᐊᑕ ᐱᕿᓐᖃᑕᐅᖥᕿᑕ. ᖁᑭᖅᖃᕐᓂ
ᐊᖅᐸᕆᐊᖃᖅᒍᓂᖅ ᓇᐸᕿᖅᑕ ᖁᑯᕿᑎᑕᐅᕆᐊᕿᑐᓂ
ᑭᕿᐊᓐ ᑕᖄ ᐃᓄᖃ ᑐᖅᖃᖄᐊᕿᖥᐃᑕ ᐊᖃᕂᖅᑕ, ᑕᐃᒪ ᑕᖄ
ᐃᓄᖥ ᓕᖃᖄᕿᕿᖅᑐᖅ.

ᑕᖄ ᐃᓄᖅᑭᒍᐊᒍᖥ ᖁᑕᖅᖃᖥ ᖁᑭᖅᖃᕿᖅᓂᒻᖄ. ᑕᐃᕿᐊᓇ
ᖁᑭᖅᖃᓕᖃᖄᐊᔭᖄ ᓕᖃᖄᕿᕿᖅᑐᖅ.

High-Kick Game

When there is a lot of food and there is nothing else to do, the Inuit make up games to play.

In the high-kicking game, the pole is raised higher and higher until only one person can kick the ball. That person is the winner. Another boy is playing the hopping game. Here you hop for as long as you can. This is a contest, and whoever hops the longest wins. The other boy is doing a push-up and trying to pick a stick up with his mouth. His body must not touch the ground.

These games are fun, but they also make the body strong.

ᖅᑭᐱᖕᒧᑦ ᐃᒋᑦᑕᖅᑕᐅᓂᖅ

ᖅᑭᐱᖕᒧᑦ ᐃᒋᑦᑕᖅᑕᐅᓂᖅ ᖁᕕᐊᓇᖅᑐᖅ. ᑕᒡᕙ ᑕᓐᓇ ᓂᕕᐊᖅᓴᖅᔪᒃ ᖅᑭᐱᖕᒧᑦ ᐃᒋᑦᑕᖅᑕᐅᔪᖅ. ᐊᓄᕆᑲᑦᓚᒃᑐᖅ ᓄᔭᖏᓄᑦ. ᑕᓐᓇ ᖅᑭᑎᒍᓯᖅ ᓄᑕᖓᓄᑦ ᐱᒍᑦᑎᓐᓇᖅᑐᖅ ᑭᓯᐊᓂ ᖁᕕᐊᓇᕈᑕᐅᑐᐃᓐᓇᖅᑐᖅ.

Blanket-Toss Game

Blanket tossing is great fun. Here a girl is being tossed up in the air. The wind is blowing through her long hair. This game makes the children stronger, but it is just for fun, to have a good time.

ᐊᔭᒐᖅ

ᐃᓄᐃᑦ ᐊᔭᒐᕈᒪᑦᑕᖅᑐᐃᑦ ᓱᓇᑐᐃᓐᓇᕐᓂᑦ ᐊᒻᒪᓗ ᐆᒪᔪᖑᐊᕐᓂᑦ ᐊᒃᓗᓴᒥᑦ. ᑕᕝᕙᓂ ᐊᔾᔨᒥᑦ ᐊᔭᒐᕆᐊᓯᔪᐃᑦ ᖃᔭᕐᒥᑦ. 22-ᖑᓇᕐᓗᓂ ᐊᔭᒐᕆᐊᓚᒃ ᑭᓯᐊᓂ ᐃᓄᒃᑐᐃᑦ ᐱᐊᓚᓂᖅᓴᐅᔪᐃᑦ ᐊᑯᓂᐅᓗᐊᖕᒋᑐᒥᑦ ᐱᐊᓂᒍᓴᒪᕐᑐᑦ. 200-ᓂᑦ ᐊᔾᔨᖕᒋᑐᐃᑦ ᖃᓄᐃᑦᑐᑐᐃᓐᓇᕐᓂᑦ ᐊᒻᒪᓗ ᕿᑎᒐᒃᓴᑦ ᐊᔭᒐᕐᑕᖃᕐᑐᑦ.

The String Game

The Inuit like to make figures of things and animals with string. In this picture the boys are getting ready to make the shape of a kayak. It will take twenty-two separate steps, but the boy's fingers will move quickly and it won't take them long. In all, the people have over two hundred shapes to make and games to play with string.

ᓯᐳᑦᑕᐱᓂᕐᔭᑦ   ᐊᕐᕙᓇᕐᖕᒃᑎᑦ

ᐅᕙᓂ ᐊᑎᏒᒥ ᑕᑦᕽᐅᕐᕽᐤ ᐃᔪᓕᑲᓐᑭ ᐅᒥᕽᐅᑭᕽ ᐅᑭᐅᕽᖃᖅᒍᑎᐅᕠᐅᒐᓂᑦ ᐅᑭᐅᑦ ᐃᔪᓕᑲᓐᑦ ᑕᐃᕐᓗᓂ
ᐃᓄᐃᑦ ᓇᐃᑦᒃᑯᓄᓐᑳᑐᑦ. ᐊᒋᕽᑦᓂᑦ ᐆᒪᕐᔭᑦ ᑕᕽᑯᐊ ᔪᕈᑦ ᓇᐅᐃᑦ, ᐊᒪᕟᐃᑦ ᐅᐸᓗᖕᑦ ᖁᒥᓐᑦ
ᐱᑕᕽᕽᑎᑦᓗᑦ ᓐᑎ. ᐃᓄᐃᑦ ᐱᑕᕽᕼᑦᑦᓐᕽ ᐅᒥᕽᐅᕼᓂᑦ ᖕᔪᕽᑕᑳᕽᔪᑦᕽ ᓂᕽᑕᓂᕽᕼᒥᓂᑦ.

ᒥᔪᐊᕽᐊᕼᕼᒃ ᑕᐁᓇ ᐃᔪᓕᑲᓐᑭ ᐅᒥᕽᐅᕼᕠᑦ ᖁᐅᕽᓗᒍᕽᑲᐅᑕᒐᒪ ᐱᑕᕽᕠᐊᐅᕼᓇᕽᕽ. ᐅᑭᐅᕽ
ᐊᑕᐅᕽᑦᒥ ᓇᓂᕽᐅᑦᕽᓗᕽᐊᕼᕽ ᖁᖁᕽᒥᕽ ᐱᐊᔪᐊᕼᓂᕽᕼᑦ ᐅᒥᕽᐅᕼᕠᑦ ᐅᑭᐅᕽᖃᑦᒍᒥ. ᑕᐊᒪ ᓪᐁᓇ
ᐱᕽᓚᕽᐅᕽᕽ ᑐᕐᐊᒍᒥ.

Ancestral Hunters

This picture is about the woolly mammoth, thousands of years ago when the Inuit were not very tall. There was no caribou, no polar bear. There wasn't any wolf and there wasn't any dog. So the people have trapped a woolly mammoth in a pit and they are killing it, because there is nothing to eat. When I painted this woolly mammoth, I just knew it was there. Then, one year later, they found a frozen baby woolly mammoth from the Ice Age up in the Northwest Territories, and right now they have it here in Toronto.

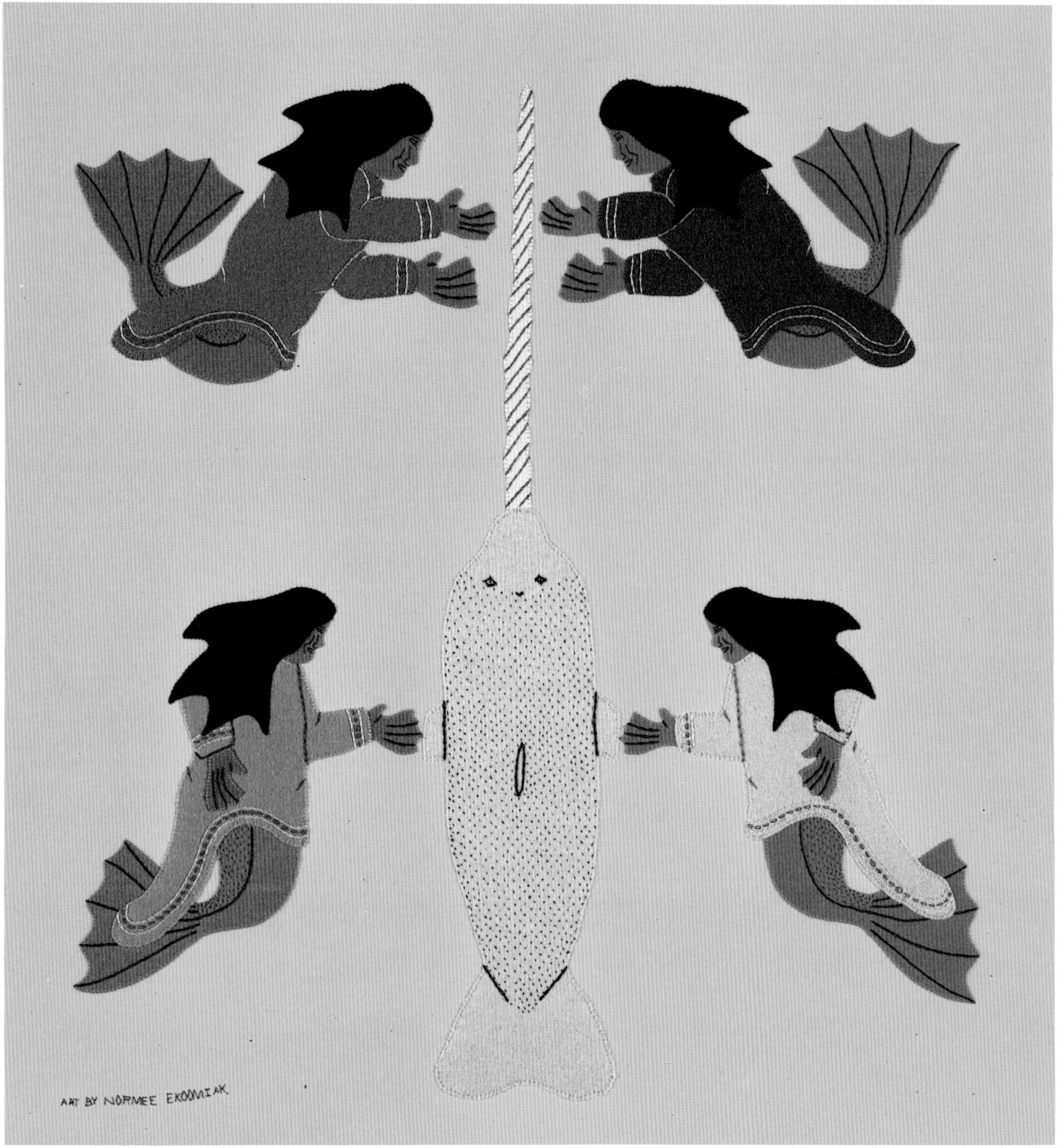
ART BY NORMEE EKOOMIAK

ᐊᕐᓇᕐᔪᐃᓐᓇᐃᑦ ᐊᒻᒪᓗ ᑑᒑᓕᒃ

ᐊᕐᓇᕐᓗᒃ ᑕᑲᓐᓈᓗᒃ, ᐃᒪᕐᒥᑦ ᑲᒪᔨ ᑕᓐᓇ ᐊᕐᓇᕐᓗᒃ ᐊᒻᒪᓗ ᑕᓐᓇ ᓇᔭᖏᑦ ᐃᒪᕐᒥᑦ ᑲᒪᔩᐅᔪᑦ. ᐊᕐᓇᑦᓗᒃ ᑕᑲᓐᓈᓗᒃ ᐱᖑᖕᑎᕐᓯᓚᐅᖕᐳᖕ ᐅᓛᒧᓗᒃᑖᓂᑦ ᐃᒪᕐᒥᑐᓗᒃᑖᓂ.

ᐊᕐᓇᕐᔪᐃᓐᓇᖕ ᐱᕐᓗᒃᓯᓱᖕᑎᖕᑎᓚᑦ ᑕᓄᐅᒥᐅᑕᕐᓂᑦ ᐊᖑᓇᓱᒃᐸᒃᑐᓂᑦ.

Mermaids and the Narwhal

We believe that just off Cape Jones, a long time ago, a father threw his daughter over the side of a boat. She was frightened and held on to the side of the boat. So her father cut off her fingers. She sank to the bottom of the water, where she became the Sedna, the sea goddess who is now a mermaid. All of the animals of the sea—the fish and the polar bear and the seal and the narwhal—were created from her cut-off fingers.

Sometimes it is dangerous in the water. A polar bear can swim out too far and then Sedna must help him back to shore. She cannot use her hands, because her fingers have been chopped off. Sedna uses her mind to make the animal turn back toward shore. The skin of the narwhal is soft and smooth. Sedna touches it and plays with it and rubs it. That is because the narwhal, who is like a king, is her son.

The mermaids will not bother people who go hunting on the sea. But if the people kill the wrong animal—anything that is on land, like wolf, fox, rabbit, ptarmigan—the mermaid will not help them. Because these people did the wrong thing, the mermaids could kill them if they wanted.

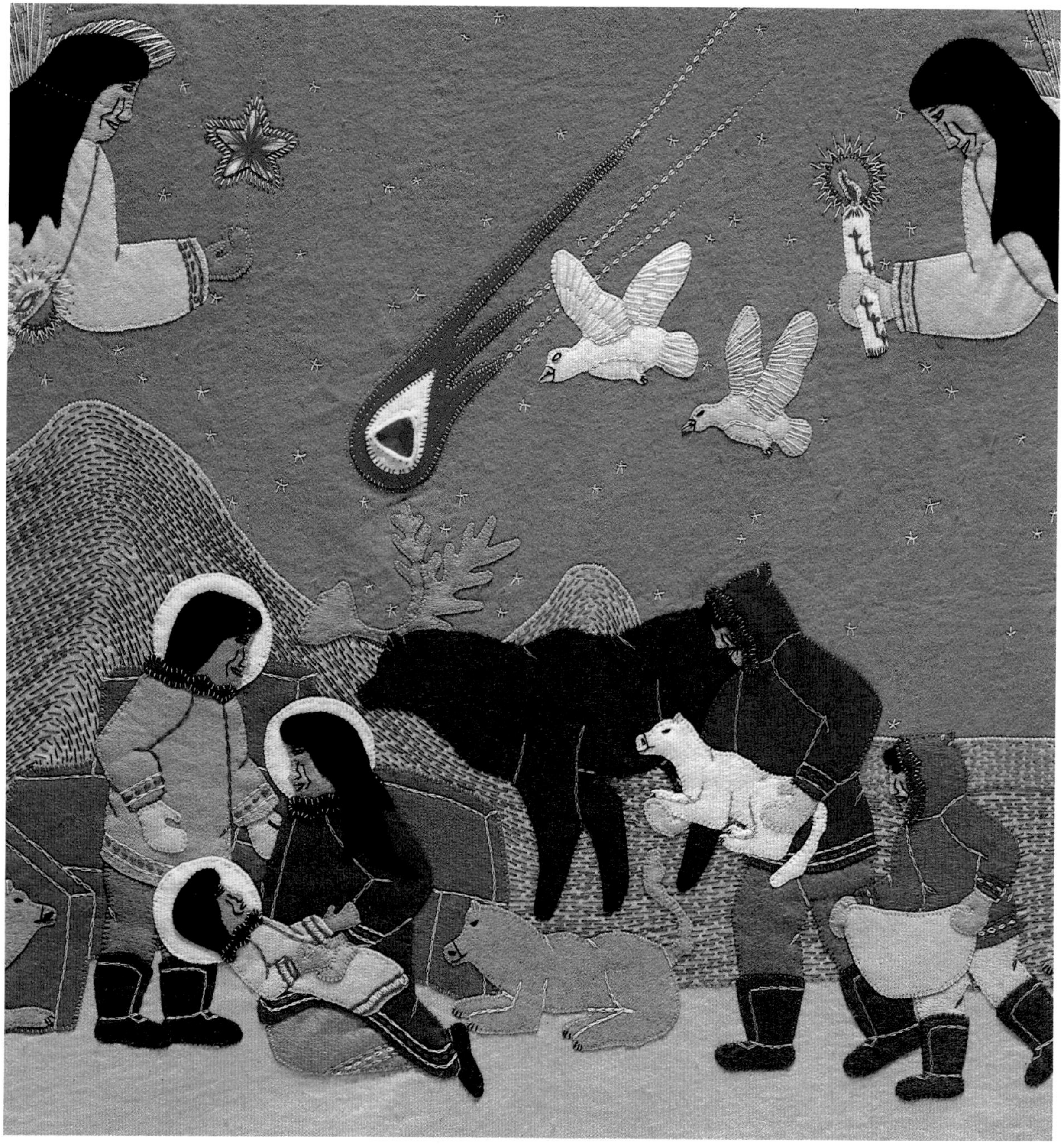

ᑯᕋᐃᔅᑐᓯᐅᑉ ᐃᕐᓂᐊᖕᒍᓂᖕᒐ
(ᐋᕐᑭᓯᒪᓂᖕᒐ)

ᐃᓄᐃᑦ ᐅᒃᐱᕐᑐᓪᓗᑎᒃ. ᐃᖕᒥᖕᓂᒃ ᐅᒃᐱᓇᔭᕐᑲᓗᑎᒃ ᐊᒻᒪᓗ ᓂᖕᑐᐃᔪᓯᕐᑲᓗᑎᒃ ᓄᓇᒥᐅᑕᓄᑦ ᐃᓄᔾᔪᑎᑭᔭᒥᖕᓄᑦ ᒥᐊᓂᕆᔭᐅᓂᖕᒐᓄᑦ. ᒫᓇ ᐃᓚᖕᑎᑦ ᐃᓄᐃᑦ ᐃᒃᓯᕋᔪᐊᕐᒥᐅᑕᐅᓪᓕᕐᓗᑎᒃ, ᐳᕋᓯᔅᑎᓐᖕᑐᓪᓗᑎᒃ, ᐅᐸᓗᓐᓃᑦ ᐸᕼᐊᐃᖕᒍᓪᓗᑎᒃ. ᑕᓐᓇ ᐅᒃᐱᓇᒐᒃᑯ ᓂᑲᖕᒐᔪᓕᐊᖕᒍᔪᒥ ᓱᓕᓂᖕᒐᓄᑦ.

Nativity (detail)

The Inuit are a very religious people. We have our own religion, and we worship the spirits of nature who protect us. At the same time, we are Roman Catholic or Anglican or Protestant or even Baha'i. I believe that what is in this picture is true.

ᐊᕐᐃᑐᓯᑎᐅᑉ ᐃᕐᓂᐊᕝᔪᓂᕐᖕ

ᐅᖅᐱᕆᖃᑉᐳᖕ ᑕᐊ ᓄᑕᕋᖅ ᔭᓯ ᐃᓄᑕᐅᓯᓂᖕ ᑕᐊ ᐱᕐᖕᑎᒋᓗ ᐊᖕᐱᒐᖕᓂᖕᕿ ᑲᑎᖕᒃᕞᐊᕐ
ᐃᓄᐃᕝ ᔾᕝᕢᖕᔾᒥ. ᐅᕞᓯ ᓄᑕᕋᖅ ᔭᓯ ᐃᓄᓯᖕᓗᕐ. ᐃᓄᐃᕝ ᐊᐃᖕᔾᖅᖕᔭᐃᕐ ᔪᓂᔾᕐᐊᖕᓂᓯᕢ,
ᐱᐅᖕᖅᕤᕐᐊᕧᑎᖕᖕᓗᕢ, ᔥᓂᑕᐅᕝ ᔥᖕᖕᓂᓗᕢ, ᖅᕞᖕᓂᕝ ᐊᖕᒐ ᖕᕝᕝᕐ ᐊᖕᔪᓗᕣᐊᕫᑎᕞᕢ. ᑕᐊ ᖅᓗᕐᖕ
ᐊᖕᒐ ᓂᓯᕐᕗ ᐱᐊᕚᖕᖕ ᒣᐊᕐᕙᕞᕣᖕᕢᕢ.

ᑕᐊ ᐃᕝᓂᐊᕝᔪᓂᖕᕞ ᐊᓲᓇᐃᖕᕐᑕᖅ ᐅᕞᓴᐊᕝ ᖕᒪᐊᕞᓇᐅᕞᕢ. ᒪᕚᖕᖕ ᐅᖕᐃᕝ ᐊᖕᒐ ᒪᕚᖕᖕ ᐊᓇᕞᖅ
ᐱᐊᕙᖕᕢᖕ, ᓂᒐᒥᐊᕝᔾᕢ ᓇᕝᕝᖅᒪᕢ ᒥᐊᓇᖕᕽᕢᕢ ᓄᖕᕞᕢ ᔭᔾᕣᕢ. ᑕᐊᓗ ᐊᒐᒃᖅ ᕿᕢᒥᖕ ᔾᕚᓇᖕᔾᒥᕢ
ᓂᖅᕞᖕᔾᖅ ᑕᕧᒧᕢ. ᔾᕞᖅᕤᕝᐊᕫᒥᖕᓗᖕᕝ ᐊᕝᕢᓂᕢ ᐃᓂᖕᕢᕢ ᐊᖕᒐ ᓯᕞᕣᖕᕞᖕᓂᕢ
ᑕᐊᕝᕤᕝᕞᕫᖕᓗᖕᕝ ᓄᑕᕞᕞ ᔭᔾᕣᕢ.

Nativity

I believe that a Baby Jesus is born everywhere, to every different group of people in the world. Here Jesus is a baby Inuk. The people are bringing him their gifts, good luck charms: a narwhal tusk, a blanket, and a spear for hunting. The dog and the polar bear cub are there to watch over him and protect him.

Up in the sky the North Star and a great shooting star are signs of the miracle. Two snowy owls and two angels, with candles from the church, are there to watch and protect. The wolf on the hill is howling the good news to the moon, and it will be heard by more people, more children, and more wild animals, who will all come to Baby Jesus.

ᓕᐳᕐᑎᐅᑉ ᐱᓂᖅᑲ

ᑕᓐᓇ ᒥᖕᓯᓚᐅᕐᐸᕋ ᓂᕕᖅᑲᔪᓚᐊᖕ ᑐᓂᓴᓯᐅᕐᑯᓪᓗᒍ ᐃᓄᓗᒃᑖᓂᑦ ᐅᑭᐅᖕᑕᖕᑐᒥᐅᑕᓂᑦ ᑕᕐᓯᒧᖅᑲ ᓕᐳᕐᑎᒧᑦ 100-ᓂᑦ ᓇᓪᓕᐅᑎᓂᖅᑲᓄᑦ. ᐊᔾᔨᒋᖕᒋᑐᐃᑦ ᑲᓚᖅᒋᑦ ᑎᖅᒥᐊᑦ ᑐᑭᖃᖕᑐᑦ ᐊᔾᔨᒋᖕᒋᑐᐃᑦ ᑭᓇᒃᑯᑐᐃᓐᓇᐃᑦ ᐃᓄᐃᑦ ᐅᑭᐅᖕᑕᖕᑐᒥ ᐊᒥᐊᓕᑲᓄᖅᑲᐅᓂᖅᑲᑦ ᑲᒪᒍᓯᒋᐊᕐᑐᕐᓗᑎᒃ ᓕᐳᕐᑎᒥᑦ ᐊᒻᒪᓗ ᖁᕕᐊᓯᒋᐊᑐᕐᓗᑎᒃ. ᑕᓐᓇᓗ ᐅᒃᐱᒃ ᐅᐃᒪᐃᓴᒋᐊᕐᑐᖕᑐᖕ ᓕᐳᕐᑎᒥᑦ, ᐅᒃᐱᐅᑉ ᐱᓂᖅᑲ, ᑕᐅᑐᒃᑐᖕ ᓇᓂᑐᐃᓐᓇᕐᓂᑦ ᐊᒻᒪᓗ ᓱᓇᓗᒃᑖᓂᑦ.

The Spirit of Liberty

I made this wall hanging as a gift from the native people of North America when the Statue of Liberty was one hundred years old. The different-colored geese flying by stand for all of the races of man. They have all come to North America to enjoy liberty and happiness. Watching over them and the Statue of Liberty is Okpik, the spirit owl, who sees everywhere and who sees everything.

The Inuit

There are approximately a hundred thousand Inuit, or Eskimos, in the world today. Some live in Greenland (Denmark), some in Siberia (the Soviet Union), and some in Alaska (the United States). In Canada there are twenty- to twenty-five thousand Inuit. Most of them live in the part of the country known as the High Arctic. It is a region of snow, ice, and rock, swept by dry winds and dangerous blizzards. There are no roads or big cities. Yet the Inuit have managed to survive and prosper in this environment.

Traditional Inuit were hunters and trappers. They built houses of snow and ice in the winter, and tents of animal hide in summer. They went where game was most plentiful.

Many people think that Eskimos still live in iglus and travel only by dogsled. Some do, but most have incorporated modern housing and vehicles like snowmobiles into their lifestyle as well. On a hunting trip, for instance, both a snowmobile and a dogsled might be used—the dogsled because it will not run out of gas, and the snowmobile because it can go faster. Modern Inuit life is often a mixture of the old and the new.

Among the Inuit there are many different groups, called bands, tribes, or nations. Each of these groups lives in a different territory; each has its own language dialect and its own culture. Some of these groups are the Mackenzie, or Inuvialuit; Copper; Netsilik; Caribou; Iglulik; and Ungava.